A Gift
for
Grandma
Holly

Written By Patti Ostrander   Illustrated By Nikki Milley

A Gift for Grandma Holly
Copyright 2020 by Patti Ostrander

Published by Patti Ostrander, Buffalo, New York
Cover and Interior Design by Nikki Milley

Printed by IngramSpark

Ostrander, Patti, 2020
A Gift for Grandma Holly
ISBN 978-1-7333848-2-7

A portion of the proceeds from the sale of this book will be donated
to Golisano Children's Hospital CICU in Rochester, NY.

This book is dedicated to my firstborn grandson, Judah, who has given us more hope and joy than we could have ever known. To my mother, without her I never would have had my own "gift" to remember her by.

A heartfelt "thank you" to Lisa Varco and Shirley Genovese, who stood by me and encouraged me to keep at it. You helped me to understand and do things that I never thought I could do!

To my children, who were so glad that I was finally finishing this book!

Emily loved to run on the sand along the
water's edge and watch the waves take away her
footsteps.

She sat down and noticed how the sand sparkled in the sunlight like glitter, and remembered how her Grandma Holly loved glitter.

Suddenly Emily was saddened by the memory of her grandma who passed away only months ago.

She was her best friend in the whole world. "I miss her so much," Emily said out loud. She kicked the sand with her foot as warm tears dripped down her cheeks and cried, "I hate that she isn't here anymore! It's just not fair!"

Grandma Holly had taken Emily to the beach on her tenth birthday, and taught her how to dig for things buried in the sand. She and Grandma had made many things from surprises they had found.

They found many treasures together. It seemed so long ago, but it was only last year. Now Emily would have to find them by herself.

Emily and her family had moved to Grandma Holly's house right on the ocean beach. It was hard at first for her because of all the things that were left behind, and Emily refused to go into grandma's bedroom.

She could smell her flowery perfume outside the door and would not go in. She kind of wanted to forget all about it, because it made her heart ache.

Sometimes they found sand dollars and sometimes little crabs that had buried themselves. Emily loved to watch the little crabs scatter over the sand and then hide again.

Emily thought she could make something very special in memory of Grandma Holly so everyone would look at it and think of her. After thinking for a while, Emily got the best idea ever.

She would make a beautiful Christmas ornament out of a sand dollar. Sand dollars were grandma's favorite sea shell. She knew that it might be difficult to find the size she would need.

Emily remembered Grandma Holly saying, "When the tide goes out and the beach is big, look for little holes in the wet sand and dig there."

Emily began her search but noticed that the tide was coming in and grumbled, "Now I will have to start my search tomorrow."

The next morning, Emily woke up, jumped out of bed and looked out the window. "Good, the tide is out," she whispered to herself.

She put on her blue shorts and white and red striped
shirt that grandma had given her and ran downstairs.

When she got to the beach, she started looking for little holes in the sand and found none. She was losing her patience and began feeling cranky. She continued looking at the sand looking for a clue showing her where to dig.

Finally, she saw the little holes Grandma Holly taught her to look for in the sand. She began digging and found two small sand dollars. They were nice but not big enough. "I'll just keep looking until I find what I want," she complained.

Emily was prepared to search all day, then she noticed the dark clouds swiftly coming toward her.

The rain came fast and hurt when it struck her face. She shut her eyes. She couldn't see where she was going and started to cry. It began to thunder and it terrified her. She didn't know what to do.

She thought if Grandma Holly had been with her, she wouldn't be so afraid. Then, she opened her eyes and saw a small wooden rowboat upside down not too far from her. She ran over to it and tucked herself beneath it.

When the rain stopped, she was able to get out from underneath the boat and walk home.

Emily was so disappointed that she couldn't go back out to the beach and finish her search. She was anxious to get her special surprise done in time for Christmas, which was only weeks away. She just sat and stared out the window at the water and the waves.

Emily became bored and wandered upstairs, stopping at her grandmother's old room. She hadn't gone in that room since before Grandma Holly left. It had been just so hard for her. Today was different.

Emily walked close to the door and placed her hand on the doorknob quickly pulling it away. She put her hand on the doorknob again and found herself opening the door.

As she looked into the room she saw all of grandma's
pretty things and smelled the wonderful scent of
of her grandmother.

She walked across the room to the closet, turned on the light and walked in. There were so many familiar clothes hanging in there and in the corner, on the floor, were boxes piled on top of one another.

She carefully inspected each one, until she got to the bottom of the pile.

There on the bottom of the pile stood a beautiful box taped shut with a beautiful ribbon wrapped around it. Under the ribbon there was a note that said, "For Emily."

Emily opened the box and it was full of sand. "Why would grandma have a box of sand in her closet?" she thought, "and then she left it for me."

Putting her hand down into the sand, she felt something and grabbed it. She pulled out her hand and in it was the most beautiful, big sand dollar she had ever seen!

She had tears in her eyes because she had found exactly what she needed. It made her so happy!

She brushed off the sand and took the sand dollar to the craft table by the window where she and grandma used to make things together. She picked out red and green paint, clear glitter, and a red velvet ribbon. Underneath she found a paintbrush.

She painted a picture of green holly leaves and red holly berries on the front of it. Then she sprinkled the glitter on the wet paint so it would stick. Last, she took the ribbon and pulled it through a hole at the edge of the shell.

Emily really didn't want to decorate the Christmas tree with her family because Grandma Holly always came to their house every year to help decorate the tree. She sat in her room staring at the ornament she had made.

Eventually Emily went downstairs and placed the special ornament right on the front of the tree so everyone could see it. She knew how much grandma would have loved it. The whole family said it made them feel like Grandma Holly was right there with them. What a wonderful gift for all to share!

Emily smiled so wide that it made her cheeks hurt. "I never thought that the sand dollar I dug for all over the beach was hidden up in grandma's closet," she thought while looking at the tree.

As Emily continued staring at the ornament on the Christmas tree, she really missed her grandma, but she also felt warm and cozy. She smiled, she wasn't sad anymore.

Grandma Holly often said, "Sometimes when you are so eager to find something and cannot find it, maybe, just maybe, you will find it in the most peculiar place."

ABOUT THE AUTHOR

Patti is a retired nurse, empathetic, and lover of laughter. Grandmother of six, she adores children and likes to make up stories with them. She studied Special Education at Morehead State University in Kentucky, and attended Buffalo General School of Nursing in Buffalo, NY.

"If I can help one child walk through the valley of grief, I will be satisfied."

In "A Gift for Grandma Holly," she portrays a young girl, Emily, who has recently lost her best friend, Grandma Holly. Emily is angry and heartbroken, but finds a way to make grandma a wonderful gift in her memory for Christmas. The gift turns out to be a gift for someone else too.

ABOUT THE ILLUSTRATOR

Nikki Milley is an award-winning portrait artist and illustrator with a wide range of experience in creating visual arts in charcoal, graphite, colored pencil, and watercolor. She has recently received recognition for her latest works, which showcase both her childlike imagination and her technical excellence depicting scenes that are at once whimsical and hyper-realistic.

Her works can be found in private collections as well as group exhibitions throughout WNY. She works from her art studio in Wilson, NY.

CPSIA information can be obtained
at www.ICGtesting.com
Printed in the USA
LVHW060809081220
673551LV00003B/163

9 781733 384827